Teaching people of all ages to
respect the earth's fragile environment,
the Minnesota Zoo is internationally
recognized as a leader in protecting
and breeding endangered
and threatened species.

A Walk Through The Minnesota Zoo was adapted from
A Walk Through The Woods Of Minnesota by G J & B Publishing.

Editorial assistance: Tom Stein and Anita Jenssen

Please write with comments or requests:
G J & B Publishing
P.O. Box 3301
Minneapolis, Minnesota, 55403

Library of Congress Registration No. Pending
ISBN: 0-9635006-1-9
First Printing: November 1993
Printed in the United States of America
Printed By Gopher State Litho, Minneapolis, Minnesota
Printed on Acid Free Paper

Other G J & B Publications:
A Walk Through The Woods Of Minnesota
available at fine stores everywhere. Ask for it!

A Walk Through
The Minnesota Zoo

Rhythmic jumps of dolphins,
intricate markings of the tiger and
kaleidoscopic colors of tropical fish
represent some of the beauty you will
encounter in a walk through the
Minnesota Zoo. With our protection,
each species will be passed through
the generations like a precious gem
to be treasured.

Ocean Trail

Dolphins

Jumping in a perfect arch
and leaving a slight wave,
the dolphin curves and slides
deeper into the water. Undulating from
head to tail, he appears to swim effortlessly
with his companions by his side. Having natural
sonar ability, dolphins are sensitive
to impulses in their environment.
They are endearing creatures
and many audiences are
captivated by them.

Tropics Trail

Coral Reef Exhibit

As I rounded the corner, I came upon
one of the most colorful and magical exhibits
of the Minnesota Zoo, the coral reef.
Hundreds of fish in many colors and shapes
swim in schools in the gigantic tank.
It's fun to watch the zoo staff
feeding the fish their specially-made
green cubes of food. I really enjoyed
looking at the pristine water and coral
as my imagination took me
on a journey to the depths
of the South Pacific.

Malayan Sun Bear

At home in the Asian forest
is the smallest of the eight
bear species, the Malayan sun bear.
He has short dark fur and a distinctive
yellow-tinted marking on his chest.
The docile sun bear is a skilled
climber and has a diet favoring
insects, small fruits and roots
of the rain forest.

Minnesota Trail

Beaver

Peeking out from the lodge, the beaver
enjoys a quick break from his arduous work.
From the viewing window, I watched
the beaver family swim around their
lodge. Gnawing on twigs and
slapping mud with paddle-shaped
tails, the lifestyle of the beaver
is demonstrated very well.

Lynx

High above, by a rocky crag,
the lynx is perched. Looking much
like his relative the bobcat, he has
pronounced tufted ears. The lynx
has large padded feet which are perfectly
designed for walking atop snow.
With gray, soft fur he blends
well with the natural beauty
of Minnesota.

Northern Trail

Timber Wolf

On the Northern Trail,
the timber wolves are viewed in
their natural habitat. I immediately
noticed their thick fur and realized they are
prepared for harsh climates and are
camouflaged with the natural colors
of the woods. The shy and reclusive
timber wolf stands three feet tall
and five feet long.

Moose

With large, flattened antlers
overhead, the long-legged moose
saunters through foliage
browsing for food. Velvety brown
from rack to hoof, the moose is the
largest member of the deer family.
Found in northern regions,
it adapts well to cold climates
and marshy terrains.

Tiger

As the tiger appears from behind
the rocks, its power is immediately felt.
It swipes its large paws and with precise
gentleness licks them to groom its fur.
The tiger has a broad face and
neck and is very colorful
with its orange and
black striped fur.

Pronghorn Antelope

Nestled among the grasses,
the pronghorn are nicely silhouetted.
The shy pronghorn can weigh
over 100 pounds and grow
to nearly five feet in length.
The white patch on their
hindquarters is unmistakable.
The pronghorn is the only horned
mammal that sheds the outer
covering of its horns yearly.

Koala

Searching through the
eucalyptus trees, I spotted the
furry koala, slowly chewing his
dinner. A black nose and tufted
ears detail this charming marsupial
(pouched animal) of Australia.
In studying the exhibit
information, I learned koala
means "the animal
that does not drink."

Zoolab

One of my most enjoyable stops at the zoo
is the Zoolab. I love to touch the
hard, bony-covered armadillo and stick
my hand in the cool water to feel the starfish.
Sometimes I even get to touch the smooth skin
of one of the big snakes. And I'm really
glad the zoo has the vibrant toucan, because it
represents all the colors of the artist's palette.
I even discovered that the woodpecker and
the toucan are cousins. The Zoolab,
filled with species from all corners of the
globe, is a great source of
information and is always a
favorite stop on my walk
through the Minnesota Zoo.

Animal Tracks

Match the animals to their tracks.

Answers at the bottom of page.

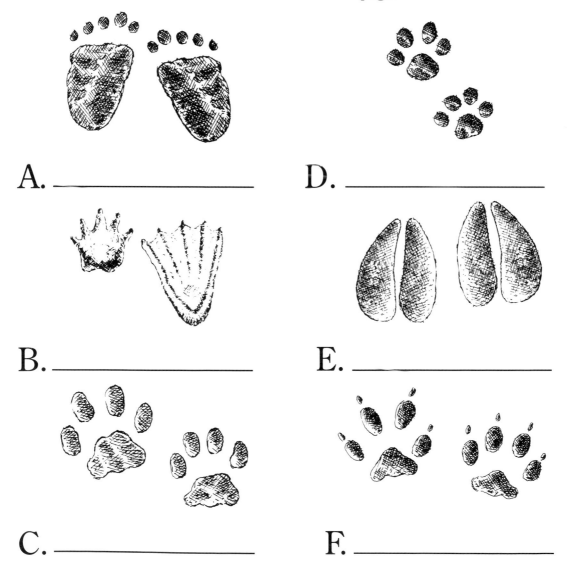

A. _____

D. _____

B. _____

E. _____

C. _____

F. _____

Inspirations

Our Trip To The Minnesota Zoo

You will meet many animals while walking the Minnesota Zoo Trails. Discover the different varieties of animals in their natural environments.

Day _____   Month _____   Year _____

_____Dolphins   _____Timber Wolf

_____Tropical Fish   _____Moose

_____Malayan Sun Bear   _____Tiger

_____Beaver   _____Pronghorn Antelope

_____Lynx   _____Koala

_____Trumpeter Swan   _____Hornbill

_____Bali Mynah   _____

_____   _____

_____   _____

Be sure and stop by the Children's Zoo and meet these fun animals:

_____Potbelly pig   _____Donkey

_____Reindeer   _____Goat

_____Goose   _____Duck

_____Llama   _____Rabbit

Join The Zoo

It's one of the best family values in Minnesota! As a member of the Minnesota Zoo, you'll enjoy unlimited free admission for a year, the Zoo's publication mailed to your home, gift store discounts, members' only events, reciprocity with over 90 other zoos across the country and more.

$30 Individual Membership
One person named on membership card

$35 Individual Plus
One person named on membership card PLUS one free guest each visit

$45 Household
Maximum of two named adults residing at the same address and their children and/or grandchildren under 18 years of age

$60 Household Plus
Same as Household membership PLUS one free guest each visit.

$100 Advocate
Same as Household membership PLUS two free guests each visit.

Just send your membership fee along with your name and complete address to:

Minnesota Zoo Membership
13000 Zoo Boulevard
Apple Valley, MN 55124-8199

or call (612) 431-9304

"A Walk Through The Minnesota Zoo"
is dedicated with love and thanks
to the following friends and families.

Lucinda McCandless
The Holzer Family
Erik Allstot
Alexandra Jeanne Hiniker
Joey Hafner
Brian Hafner
The Balcoms
Nathan Balcom
Howie Lambert
Peter Erdahl
Brett Shanley
The Endres Family
David Spence
The Davies Family
Gregory Bowman
Aaron Louis Davies
Stefanie Weisenburger
John Corbo
Tyler Thompson
Erin Lee Thompson
Kelsi Roth
Keith Wallace
Joshua Koslowski
Sean Smith
Olivia Martinetti
Emma Rosemary Harrington
Jonathan Parker
Laura Jacobson
Sara Rockwell
Mark Rockwell
Alexander Hannan
Wendy Jean Schneider
The Keyler Family
Cody Wubben
Bradley Wubben
Kenneth G. Teachout

Samantha Giese
Ryan Giese
Jonathan Gould
Duncan Haney
Chris Thompson
Nick Thompson
Courtney Thompson
Marian L Melich
Gene & Linda Taylor
Eddie & Jean Fuerstenberg
Brian Jon Fuerstenberg
Bob & Shirl Smith
Milt & Phyllis Daline
William & Kathleen Vanderbilt
Dick & Beverly LeVoir
Jessica Kerr
April & Jim Sunderlin
Peter Grinsell
Ray Fuerstenberg
Stewart & Jean Montgomery
Mary & Katie Montgomery
Adeline Gangelhoff
Phil Gangelhoff
Tom & Shirley Gangelhoff
Wendy Watson
Sachi Watson
Gerald B. Johnston
David M. Jelle
Jerome V. Deiley
Kathleen Berger
Anthony R. LaPoint
Freyja Hafner
Tristan Hafner
Alexander Scott Nord
Mercedes Rose Pitzer

Amanda & Zachary Castonguay
Sandy Schroeder
In memory of Leonard Melich
In memory of Carl & Amilia Wolfe
The Bud Belk family
Jim & Chris Haines
John & Joni Belk
"Sportsfan" Belk
Bill & Phyllis Ptak
Harold & Cleo Belk
Bob & Susan Hylland
Gordy & Jennifer Skaar
Peter G. Haines
Don & Lucy Opsahl
Bob & Nina Roseland
Irv & Mary Jean Dahlstrom
Rachel Adkins
Megan Myhre
Olivia Wilson
Alec Wilson
Ryan Reule
Jana Reule
Megan Reule
Tommy Anderson
Kyle Burdick
Alexandra Elizabeth Tillotson
Cole Christian Jensen
Katherine Lee Pemberton
In memory of Rhoda Schwandt Mooers
In memory of Vida Belk
In memory of Ethel Belk
In memory of Irma Belk Hobart
In memory of John & Jennie Belk
In memory of Vernon & Eva Belk
In memory of Jewell & Mary Tarver